meme

KUHL HOUSE POETS
edited by Mark Levine

meme

poems by

Susan Wheeler

University of
Iowa Press,
Iowa City

University of Iowa Press, Iowa City 52242

www.uiowapress.org
Printed in the United States of America

Design by Barbara Haines

The University of Iowa Press is a member of Green Press Initiative and is committed to preserving natural resources.

Printed on acid-free paper

Library of Congress Cataloging-in-Publication Data

Wheeler, Susan, 1955–
Meme: poems / by Susan Wheeler.—1st ed.
p. cm.—(Kuhl House poets)
ISBN-13: 978-1-60938-127-1 (pbk)
ISBN-10: 1-60938-127-0 (pbk)
ISBN-13: 978-1-60938-142-4 (ebook)
ISBN-10: 1-60938-142-4 (ebook)
I. Title.
PS3573.H43465M46 2012
811'.54—dc23 2012004396

in memory of my mother and father

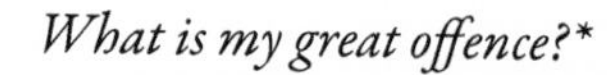

*All quotations on section title pages are from *Propertius: Elegies*, edited and translated by G. P. Goold (Cambridge: Harvard University Press, 1990).

CONTENTS

As for the poems you composed in my honour,
burn them, I pray: cease to win praise through me.

The Maud Poems

Two Shakes of a Lamb's Tail

She was a real stickler.

Well, I couldn't get it for the life of me. All I remember is, *Mademoiselle Skeen, vous êtes une tête du bois!*

> Where is there room for all I have to say
> in the deepening dark of fall's afternoon?
> Baubles, prizes, in the cereal box.

He was a trooper, but out in his neck of the woods that was what they did. The others walked around in their Skivvies all day.

It's slim pickings——Dan said you didn't want any anyway.

Fiddlesticks

Who rattled your cage? No, I do not have a Q-tip up here. Go ask your father. Wait——you're going downstairs like that over my dead body.

> In the sepulcher where the mother lay
> at last some sleep to gain,
> Hannah helped me carve the oak
> into granite with her cane.

Don't come in here all bright-eyed and bushy-tailed expecting us to give you more.

I Was Just Frosted

Thanks, Ray, this is just what the doctor ordered.

No, you never see me have one with olives——your father likes olives but I can't stand them.

No, cocktail onions are just picked small. Turn that down, Dan.

> Avocados, toothpicks. Coleus, root sprawl.
> The diffident glints of a late-day sun, rays
> splintered by leaves: they shake and, in their
> shaking, streak the light. Transparent murk
> of glasses at the glass.

Would you move just one inch over? There. The light was in my eye.

Splitting Hairs

I learned how to make ring tum ditty when your father and I didn't have two cents to rub together.

Well, these saltines are a little stale.

You don't have to finish it, but no dessert if you don't.

> You want the sound turned down, wound
> low, the dial on the dash cranked off. You
> want no utterance, and peace, and a clear,
> unwheezing breathing.

He was sick as a horse this morning but now he's just feeling a little punk.

Don't you wash that down the sink!

Wild Goose Chase

Oh dear. Would you pick that up, I dropped it.

Ray, don't make it too stiff. Myr's coming over to drop off the blueprints and she might like to join us.

He's been a real pest all afternoon so he's in the doghouse. Dan! You can come out, but watch your p's and q's or——

> Stanchion where a rope marks off the object.
> Wallpaper, striped: a slippery floor. A
> guard. In his element. Indices. And the
> long, slow tumble of snow.

Good Lord, it's hotter than Hades in here!

A Good Egg

But that was your grandmother. I knew I looked good when she said, *Cut your lip?* Ray, the dog got out. You'll have to pick off the burrs.

> Headlong onto the grass, a crow and its
> silken down drops, black bomb. Child on a
> bird's back streams like a kite.

She was sharp as a tack, always was. Can you take the hint?

Turkey in the Straw

Better get cracking. You're the one who made it an uphill battle; your brother's going great guns.

> Stasis of the street behind her, through the
> window: leaves unstirred, grass erect,
> dun dun dun distant thud of pavement-breakers
> in the noon.

I don't want to hear a word from you until you pick up steam. Now go find Minneapolis. Get lost.

Round Robin Hood's Barn

It's all right, Ray, she's already spilled the beans.

You think you can? Neat trick. Now you go across the street and apologize. Tell them who put number two on their fence.

Where was I? Drat. Oh, he was fudging the numbers for years. He just figured he'd get away with it by hook or by crook.

Shhhh——a cardinal, right there!

> Bird dips its head: it's an owl, recalcitrant
> in its non-hooting state. Wild billowing of
> sails beyond it. Wind-swept surging of trees.

Not one word, young lady! You've raised enough Cain for one afternoon.

She's a Pill

Oh, dangling long sleeves in the Mercurochrome.
Parking her punch on her knees.

I'm not a joiner.

In the night, a visitation, small as a thumb,
enters the sealed house and ascends.

Mother wouldn't have stood for *that* long. Drippy-drooping around on heels. Leaving the blue cheese out.

Jeehosaphat

Good grief, you don't have the sense God gave geese. I told you this morning, I won't be your chauffeur. And take that ratty thing off.

> Where the jays upset the feeder——
> under the house where Jamaica hid——
> hands in brook-water, cold——

Something wasn't quite Hoyle about the way she got that *A*. No, I don't like your just *hanging out.*

Oh, piffle. That's not what you said last night.

Johnny on the Spot

Woops. I have to go to the john for a minute.

Will you take the broccoli out of the freezer?

> Later, in the preacher's hand, the small scoop
> sparks and the water slaps the font. My
> bangs, wet.

I'd better close up shop, I'm bushed. Pick up your feet, we're going to have to call you Lightfoot the Deer. Did your father get any mail?

Canasta

Mind your own beeswax or you'll be tarred and feathered right here and now. Ray, the dog's got something in her mouth. While you're up, would you check the ham?

> You and the beast's belly, its short sleek fur,
> its odor of a world beyond the curb. The tail
> rises, the fur fans out——

No, just see what the temperature is up to. Oh, I'll do it.

That's what I was afraid of. Dan, she skunked me.

Par for the Course

Disestablishmentarianism? Look it up.

Well, get out of my light and I'll read it to you.
Disestablishmentarianism, noun.

Osa married adventure, and Horatio Hornblower
sailed the high seas; someone floated off on a
raft named *Kon Tiki*. Ben Gurion starred in *Exodus*.
Erma grew a dandelion crop.

Honey, will you hand me my lighter?

If You're Not Careful

He was kind of——well, your father called him Fred Fairy. He was a bachelor and lived in those chock-a-blocks over near the Libby's plant.

Good Lord. There's something the matter with——

> And the veil became——was becoming to——
> the makers of the glassware at the pit, and
> the makers of the glassware at the pit took
> the veil, and the molten fire parted.

Aren't you the pot calling the kettle black?

Busier Than a Cranberry Bog Merchant

Serif or sans serif; the latter will give you a cleaner line, more legible sign. Directionals made a strong sixty-cent stripe. I could have told you that.

Replenish. Replenish my glass. The crane in the cocktail onion jar. Earth Shoes giving out.

> It's the Time Machine's tunnel, and my own
> wavery voice waving back from the walls of
> its chute's what I hear. Her own's near my
> ear.

Oh, the bone's the best part. Em ess. Mouth shut.

Where'd You Come From?

If you're looking for something to eat *now*, there's cheese in the middle drawer.

No, not before dinner. I'm going to call you in fifteen minutes to set the table, so don't get involved.

Attest——ament, filament, adamant, keen.

Oh, there's nothing like horseradish with a New England boiled dinner.

Just Vanilla

She was a pistol. And he——remember him, Ray?——Ray thought he was too big for his britches. She was full of herself too but it was Colin who wanted to live high on the hog.

Your father thought she was pretty spiffy.

> In the garden the burdensome riot unfurls in the
> heat, in sun, in shade, while you lie on the bench
> in a sweat.

Well, they went bloody blue blazes through their last dollar before you could say boo.

Judas Priest

You can't sit there and tell me anything you've said here is true.

Lace our shut eyes shut.

Don't you ping my machine. Young lady.

Hot Sketch

Oh for heaven's sake. How did you know I wanted one of these?

Last time I had a dickens of a job getting it loose and then there was just one measly piece left.

> What drums behind her is the thump of the
> backhoe striped by sun in the picture window.
> The particles drift.

Well, if you'd hold it where I could see it!

I see, you're an Indian giver. Don't push your luck.

Flame

He didn't hold a candle to Meldrum Dieffenthaler, but they both made my skin crawl.

No, don't get up, I can reach it from here.

> Astonied, the cerebellum and the frontal
> cerebellum, limbs, and a mind teeters from
> sense. I would have waited if the crank
> had wound down.

Oh, he wasn't anything to write home about, either. Too stuck on himself to be much use.

Not My Bailiwick

It was nip and tuck until Gladys got seven in a row. He was miffed but that's how we had fun back then.

Get me another ice cube while you're up.

> Motored here, there, to a floating bird's carcass.
> What *bright feathers, what a talon* or *beak* said
> the rest. Often the sun came up on its shore-side,
> often it shone on its nest.

Well, that's what makes ballgames. You say potato.

Come over here in the light. There's something on your bazooms, right here, oh, it's a leaf.

Ten Conniptions

Hold your horses.

If you don't knock it off now there will be no cake for you. You're skating on thin ice.

That's it. That's the last straw. You get down off your high horse, young lady, and shape up or ship out.

Can I pack your bags?

> Yes, divided blessing: banishment, ruin.
> Dragging its lines, the trawler
> buckles under.

Such are the deadly curses my page prophesies for you:
learn to dread the end that awaits your beauty.

The Devil
—or—
The Introjects

In the intimate turn, the beloved's breath, she's suddenly there. *Whore.*

She mocks what she gives. On the diving-board edge of a shiny new pool, she's braiding a noose of your hair. The long light, the trees, the quickening air—a ladybug's whir to the crook of your arm and the soft plod of shoes coming forth from the house—the peaceable place not peaceful but hers.

Grammy. Grammy. You weren't much for names. Sorry-ass whine—no—*sorry-ass whine.* She's got your hand moving out for a dish, for a drink, for a doughnut. She's rubbing your twat with the heel of her thumb, she's eyeing your ear. Then minesweeper, hour after hour.

You've given your last to the man without thumbs but she's after you.
Give a bill, missy, then squander the rest, and she's cupping your eyes to
the crinoline shop. Pavement spins at your feet, then a corner, turn—
and a billboard rears up like a snake. *Fur.*

She wants you to break with your mom. *Go on honey. Give that bitch desserts.*

She's followed you to the café, you see her in the mirror's blink making eyes at the waiter's son: good hair, tight pants, but he's three. Give those grains of saccharin dust a stir. *Bathetic actress*, and the whisper's hers. There's a fork of her scarf that's pinned to the booth and you think may it never set free.

Careful, she's whispering, and she's following you up the street, one hand in your shoulder bag. *Careful, you vermin, you wretch, you petty cunt, careful.*

She's driven you out here with her taunting, pushed you out to the extremities of town where the dust coils in the wind and your own parched throat rasps. *Go on, missy, jump,* but the land's straight and flat, and the prefab arsenal by the side of the road bears unbankable walls. *Jump.*

Never, however long, does love last long enough.

The Split

Spangled like showgirls in the gleam of our fears,
shiny Christians in chain mail, with our faux-lizard shingling,
whores limping to West Street from the Bank Street pier,
we were wed in the chapel, ten years—
ten yrs./twenty days—before stone changed to rain,
and people, rain, too, and cinders, all, sinking.

Don't make so much—noise? money? tsouris?
Of this. The signs were there to be read?
from the start?   in our *faulty*
intelligence?

There you go. A molehill, a mound, while
the shrouded peaks of (?) *Riva's mounts*
tower, still.

The beloved sturms to his drang.
The adulterer winces at bears.
The philanderer slips him the date-rape drug.
The fishhusband shouts like a shrew.

If she's Nancy, then she's Kate. Or Sue.

Once Kate, at noon, stumbling up from bed,
knew the slip his johnson made in her slide,
or him bent over Jeremy far down the beach—

        she could only see

the small and tall from where she lay,
her feet like steles in their boots of sand, out of which
        he and Jeremy sprung.

                                        Then they were near.
Boo! she remembers, in the banging sun,
waking, Jeremy on her chest, at her ear.   And he—her
husband—a klieg, lighthouse with its back to her,
raking its view of the sea.

Now shake that. Think:

Fight over tinsel. The plumber's bill.
Fight of the unripe figs. Fight of the speaking
when, touring, lost. Fight under
overpass, in Catalan café. Method of punishment
argument; fight of the fried sister's
homecoming, amphetamines;
second-opinion scrape on the ward; fight over sharpening knives,
ways to pick cantaloupe before freak frosts descend.

Spat of

the-smell-like-cigarettes, of frittering dough until big-ticket's out;
fight on compliance with the sentence, after the conviction,
and was *straphang* a noun——

his taking pillows to the den post-the on-and-on,
curling in the tomalley light TV made, back then.

The fink was fickle.

Finkl finkl finkl
little star.

1. She was starting to look like her mother.
2. She was clingier than pantyhose.
3. He stayed out all night.
4. She liked to cuff me when she got plowed.
5. He was vapid.
6. She was a fool.
7. She ridiculed me in front of the dogs.
8. He stuck a hairpin in my ear.
9. He had an affair with my older sister.
10. He spent our money on booze and bennies.
11. She wouldn't clean and it stank like bad beef.
12. I tried to hang myself but it didn't work.
13. He didn't like my sweet potato pie and said his mother made it better.
14. She wouldn't learn trigonometry for me.
15. I took it all out on the little ones.
16. She couldn't get pregnant.
17. He was shooting blanks.
18. He made for a pitiful sight in a bathing suit.
19. I wanted out, then I didn't, then I did.
20. I just couldn't live without Sally.
21. He wanted to start a family and to start it now, with me.
22. She split when the money ran out.
23. I gave her three more chances and then I left.
24. She hated the Dave Clark Five.
25. I was indentured. I didn't know I could choose not to.
26. He went out for gum etcetera.
27. By April she had passed on.
28. He saw only his idea of me.
29. We couldn't agree on an invitation font.
30. He was bad news, and it's always, like, *bad news, here I am.*

I love her / him / them.
I'd never go back.

It's stringy   out here

in the stratosphere.

The sad night ticks like a homemade bomb.

I dream each night (in *Cancerqueen*, so many nights!) about the
churning streets, the way each person passing, in her, his surly,
individuated shoes, I didn't know but could have known.
This seeming simpler now than then.

I picked up a gal in a bar.
She said she'd ignore my cigar.
But when I was done
Relieving my gun
She said I was not up to par.

He stumbled outside to his car.
He couldn't have gotten too far.
For when I replied
Your trigger's what's died
He lit his exploding cigar.

You took a drubbing?

Yes.

You were deserving, yes?

On behalf——

Did you not follow standard operating room——

Their legs were so small. Smaller than the ring holding a cap to its bottle.

Cigarette?

No.

Grappa?

No.

They were gathering wool?

I am convinced of it, yes.

With Peter.

What?

Let's take another tack. Were your bowels——

No.

Did you misconstrue a Von's for a Spring Superette?

What?

Answer the question.

Answer the question——?

All right. Please.

No. My wife. Her umbrella. A bagatelle under the trees, a pink raised in her freckles, young mouth without crusties, my joy.

How many did you kill?

I've counted——

Yes?

None of them ever went missing.

It could have been the sea.
It could have been the stars.
It could have been
that girls not men
were the ones from Mars.

Q: What's her father's Hebrew name?

A: Her father's name is Fishl.
In her I got one kikhl
who, despite my bluff and bitl,
will keep me in the pilpl.

He drove me (~~nuts~~ ~~crazy~~ ~~bats~~)—
                    with his medicines, his cleaning jags,
his thin-band watch loose on his wrist,
his calls to his "work-friend" Peg.

I hated him like I hated lice.
Absurd, in other words: regret.

I thought I was up in my head.
Was I up in my head?
Or dead?

Times there were when we
saw love
light rooms so vast it made
us love
ourselves. You in your
lazy
leisure suit, zippered Orlon,
baby
blue, me in my hearts
peignoir——
we were a pair! Barely
coming
up for air, smearing up
a storm.
Hand over your tobacco
pouch, your

whiskey and the vindaloo.
Let's make like we're not through.

1. Anabaptists
    a. field field to
    b. lip on a / in a daisy
    c. pond muck
2. Curtailing assumptions such that
    a. frog muck
    b. panopticon the hazards
    c. signage escalator mutant tut
3. Stilt slit
    a. busker conflagration
    b. amino assets
    c. lobby here for the downtown train
4. Or: SHIT
    a. lips
    b. frog lard
    c. decently if willing

If you an ered mostly
If   partner's ans

now you   the bride

extort

compactability

makest

thou the one's beloved.

That's a pretty skirt.

Do you work here?

Are you here every day?

You have pretty hair.

I don't wear skirts.

Did you know my mother?

She might have known you, you don't know.

Hair like yours makes me want to touch it.

Okay.

I didn't mean to bother you.

Are you here every day?

I'm on this street all the time but I haven't seen you before.

What do you do when you're not here?

Your eyelashes are so light.

Did my mother have pretty hair?

Sorry. I forgot.

Briscoe, was it?
"He spends his Saturday nights punching the clown" or
"She and her pumped-up ta-tas."

Jokes the reed, in the speeding current, you cling to, at last give way.
Disaster doubles in the slightest slight.
On the fighting floor, without trainer or mouthguard, hugging one rope
then another, you see the stars bang with a roar
their circuitous augur of night on your skull.
The mind a crumble caulked with glue.
Baker's dozen, cranberry scone, bacon, eggs, ribeye, bone.

She could sweep her hair and bind it in a second's gesture.
Her silk silk hair.

The unbuckling and opening of her brassiere.

Her tiny shoulders so easily shattered. Her tiny waist.

No seam in the velvet skin. No corn borer in her silks. Small dark nails
like polished quartz.

Her foot like a child's in my palm.

Him and his dumb-ass chicklets.
His food and his "disrespecting."
His Tiparillos on the boardwalk that July.
Vagrancy. "Important calling" (his).

Ahem.

She had her trophy friends, and I wasn't one.

He said things like "good for you" and "you should think about that."

She told me I broke my arm because I wasn't ready to hold someone.

Once? When I was in traction? She put a Tareyton out on my cast.

He was a good man.

When I said zig, she said zag.

He had hair like Rapunzel.

He kissed the cats more than he kissed me.

He just kept saying to Hector you know, the scab, while I was getting ready for work, "What price?"—his eyes rolling, the whole bit.

The more I cried the more she hit me.

I can't hear you with fingers in my ears.
I can't hear me with fingers in my ears.
You don't hear me with fingers in my ears.

Double it up, my knave, my swell,
double it up, my boy——
for you'll soon forget where you put down the spoon,
you'll no longer think of the whys——but the ways
will push you clean out of the room.

At first it ruled.
Then the quiet thundered down.

Lone ship in overdrive——

Isosceles,
What did you want from me?

Now a day eclipsed——
Another night——

~~Born alone, die alone.~~

~~Be born alone, die alone.~~

~~Birth alone, die –~~

~~Arrive alone, depart alone.~~

Enter alone, exit alone.

And then the smashed ear.

Your crazy sister, your crazy mother,
your father she left to shit himself——
now you want me to join them in Denver;
let go of our fragile son, woman,
before you do him in,
let go of our beautiful son.

The girl I love lives on the canal,
not one hour from here by car;
twenty-three now there'll be because I can't
leave you alone with our son.
Done in he'll be if
you're left with our beautiful son.

Though you spin a tale about our nest
and make brass of our straw,
a child can't know the shit's *not* shit.
So, leave off—in your yarns—
our fragile son,
spare our beautiful son.

A son's a mirror of a mother's pride:
and thus the crazed outlasts
your mother, your sister, and yourself——
but not our fragile son, woman.
You'll not do him in, no,
not our beautiful son.

Imported?

’im poor *taunt*, as in ***taunt*** *what you porter in.*

Speaking of your better half,

You can be ugly and stupid as long as your shaft is big.
Be date bait for your mate.
Fried oysters ain't a euphemism.

Just get in there and see what pops up.

Okay, go your merry way.

What's her beef?

What?

So long gone had I been
that when I returned
I did not know me, the one

who called——warily, through the trees,
as I approached like a thief or a
            ground mole——*Who is it?*
I saw her whiten in the doorway,
she could have been my cousin.

                        Linda, is that you?
That's what I answered.

From the lintel she took me in, the length
of me, with my one good eye.
Nearing her, I was a worm on end, an indigent.

That was when I knew I had arrived.
The last step is the longest, impassably long, now I will always
be twinned, wanting
to not know returning.

There are pennies where the sky is falling.
The pot turns over; the copper scatters.

Henny Penny barks like an angry sow.
Her ears point like elfin ears. *Bitch-*

In-the-making, we like to call her. Pennies
Ping her head and rattle her brains.

Oh, the sky's rising! Li'l Pig cries. *I forgot*
To right-side myself! He swipes

The black flies in front of his snout
As the dark rises from land to the moon

And then wipes the ~~screen~~ scene clean.
Now Henny's braying. *Woo hoo. Woo hoo.*

Want to go watch a kibitzer crumble
In the puke-green pour of the moon?

Bye, kid in first grade on your paddle cart.

Bye, Lorraine, Outward Bound in the snow.

Bye, motorcycle David.

Bye you bright spirits, born of my friends. Jimmy. Natalie.

Bye beautiful one, your father said your pink skin would be tender, I was afraid for you.

Bye, one's devoted mother, another's devoted son.

Bye to Playboy Club Bill, to the Roxy Bill, to the Bill going aft with the cross.

Bye, dickering friend to Sonja, I wanted to show you up.

Bye Dad, bye Mom.

Bye, Duncan's dancing bear shining, shining.

Bye, great dogs I have known. Cats. Raccoon I hit.

Bye to Bob Liberty, you must be gone.

Bye to the beggar no more on his corner.

Bye Ben, sparklers and flowers, the lamp of the music.

Bye Barbara Latham, Abinata, Ray Yoshida. Bye Gelsy.

Bye Meldrum and Carrel, Gladys, Olive C. Bye May and Winslow. My lovely first cousin.

Bye to the husband who was the best wife.

Bye to those I fear dead.

I know you all in his absence tonight.

I know you all in his absence tonight.

Back in our salad days
——well, more like pb & j days
if you get my drift——you know
sticky & sweet & stuck even then——

filling——you could fill me——

The stepfather sings,

"What do I know?
I love you so.

"You were not mine yet I pine."

Canal this, canal that——
It's a Canalabaloo.
Why don't she quit her yakking?
I got to skidoo.

wait I'm not done fucking wait I'm not done fucking wait
I'm not done fucking wait I'm not done fucking wait I'm
not done fucking wait I'm not done fucking wait I'm not
done fucking wait I'm not done fucking wait I'm not done
fucking wait I'm not done fucking wait I'm not done fucking
wait I'm not done fucking wait I'm not done fucking wait

What are these things, shards between pages like blades,
        like the headless stairway struck still in rubble.

The appended flag measly, thin, flapping.

The widow asked *What should be read.*

The consultant said *Nought which consoles.*

Such is the state of our poetry caught in my throat on its way
        to my mouth, *why not do everything*

but of course we do nothing,

go nowhere, the stairs looking thin themselves, though they are made
        of the fastest iron,

measly and thin, though they are made of

the fastest iron.

Your body ups and aways (with you)
Your body ups and aways

Passive girl, impassive boy

Your body ups and aways and now it comes
Sharp to inchoate

Passive girl, impassive boy

Gazelle to gargantuan

Did you see when I gave the girl our number?
Back at Billy's Laundromat behind the bank?
Our washer, it's broke down and so I went there.
You've a right to cause me trouble now, I know.

At first I couldn't think straight, couldn't see girls
Even when they mooned me to my face.
I was so pissed at you and the fucked-up way you left,
You've a right to cause me trouble now I know.

If I had a way to make you live with me again
—Even as a rabbit, or a wren (if all that's true)—
I wouldn't see at all that girl against the wall.
You've a right to cause me trouble now, I know.

It was the winter of the Z-pack, when any Tom or Dickhead with a medical shingle repeated *viral* like a clock on the hour. I'd broken my femur—lemur?—and all the sporting ones shot the odds to *impossible, señor. Nolo posse, nolo posse*, they chanted on the hour: *just a sports sprain like the running backs get.* Are the running backs sixty-nine and three quarters? Did their wives just leave, the pickup bed clotted with every stick of furniture the two of you—them—had ever bought on time—*I think not, señor.* What I said to the last straw, some kid. If he had been mine he'd be grounded.

The eyes, going: not tragic, not
without some luck. I'll get to miss
re-enactments of the war on Fox
in spring, but even this can't top

smearing a new red nail—then,
doubling back to fix it, getting
smashed by a Prius on a wild goose
chase. Next to bloodletting going

blind is painless—no open cuts,
no broken bones, no needles—it's
muss-free slip—just muscles sore
when the eyes have strained a bit.

I *will* miss the way you look, at night—
eyes fatigued, wine-red, glum—
after you've been betrayed
by every shift I've made all day
to sight your halo against the light.

O.K. Begin in——————————love.
You're nodding.

What?

You're nutty.

Is that where

You think that it began?

If not there, where? I'd stake———

Well?

———perhaps not, after all,
but if not love, what fodder
theirs?

The garage, mine;

the kitchen hers. I err, er,
I err.

There is no knack for grief.

Had you entered the thicket in darkness,
had the brambles been swiping your face as you passed,
had you been mid-life, not in haze but in crisis,
had you no other lens but damage to gaze through,
had you—thwacked by branches—entered your true love
as your true love cried out with her palm on your face,
her heel on the small of your back in the darkness,
you might have removed the mask from your visage,
the glass from the casement, the scythe from your fist.

The bloom is off the rose: phhhhhhttt.
Botrytised? The petals fall, clump, blow.

Out in the night, a car revs
and disentangles itself
from its parking space.
I am tired. Today
I moved a book from its shelf
to the bed. The span
of its moving was vast.

We were just two drunk kids parallel parking in the dark, you saying,
Are you the one with the low down?

Under the burnt-out street lamp us kids.

Heron coasted by the house, trailing those long legs. No,
never tasted heron meat.

Dawn: through the Lincoln Tunnel the mammals
and their metal, headlighting 42nd Street. By the way,
you weren't born in Omaha.

You said your wife changed her clothes at the wedding site because
it was too cold in the car.

I heard your anecdote, I learned what was an event to you.

When will you go away,
oh piercing, piercing wind?
When will at rest I be again?
Oh sleep that will not rain on me,
oh sleep that nothing brings.

Oh, when will a face appear
that cancels full th'other?
Or will there be no more for me
of anodyne palaver?

Ruined thighs, they notify
those whose vision makes comply
th'other parts in tandem,
that no veil or candle's light there'll be
to mask the madness love can be

embroidering on drive.

When will you go away,
oh piercing, piercing wind?
When will at rest I be again?
Oh sleep that will not rain on me,
oh sleep that nothing brings.

ACKNOWLEDGMENTS

Poems from this collection have appeared in *Drunken Boat, The Literary Review, The New Yorker, Salt, The Nation*, and *The Best American Poetry.*

I am immensely grateful to David Trinidad for help with the manuscript, as I am to Lisa Furmanski, Charlotte Wright, Claudia Rankine, Darcey Steinke, and C. K. Williams. Thank you, thank you to Jonathan Furmanski for the cover photograph.

KUHL HOUSE POETS

Oni Buchanan
Must a Violence

Michele Glazer
On Tact, & the Made Up World

David Micah Greenberg
Planned Solstice

John Isles
Ark

John Isles
Inverse Sky

Bin Ramke
Airs, Waters, Places

Bin Ramke
Matter

Michelle Robinson
The Life of a Hunter

Robyn Schiff
Revolver

Robyn Schiff
Worth

Rod Smith
Deed

Cole Swensen
The Book of a Hundred Hands

Cole Swensen
Such Rich Hour

Tony Tost
Complex Sleep

Susan Wheeler
Meme

Emily Wilson
The Keep